# TORCH

# TORCH

## POEMS

## KIM JACOBS-BECK

Wolfson Press

The author gratefully acknowledges the editors of the following magazines, in which the following poems first appeared, sometimes in slightly different versions:

*Bright Sleep Magazine*: "Michigan Women"; *NILVX*: "Card Zero: The Fool"; *Muddy River Poetry Review*: "Berry Patch" and "Observatory"; *The Apple Valley Review*: "Torch," "Easter Egg," and "Upper Midwest Love Poem"; *Thank You for Swallowing* (special American election edition): "Monday"; Love and Ensuing Madness Collection at *Rat's Ass Review*: "Skin" and "First"; *Roam Literature*: "Rumpelstiltskin."

Cover design by Sky Santiago,
based on a concept by Pedro Rubio
Interior design by Pedro Rubio
Volume editor, Nancy Botkin

ISBN: 9781950066025

Wolfson Press
Master of Liberal Studies Program
Indiana University South Bend
1700 Mishawaka Avenue
South Bend, Indiana 46634-7111
WolfsonPress.com

for Dan

# Contents

# Introduction

The poems in this short collection are love poems of one sort or another. For Jacobs-Beck, love, like nature, can be a balm, but it is also dark and dangerous, and whether romantic or familial, love is difficult and uncertain. Nevertheless love is a terrain that must be traversed and negotiated; it is steady and ever-present like her beloved mid-western landscapes. In "Back Home" a familiar lake is inextricably linked to the past, and the natural world seduces much like a lover. She begins,

> I can feel the lake before I see it
> Smell ripples in the wavelight
> Hear kelp, feel brown lapping
> At the edge . . .

The speaker's senses are engaged, and she feels pleasure deeply. However, one pleasure is matched by other tactile, less pleasant sensations. In "Skin," two lovers lie together in the dark. Her gorgeous simile:

> My silent anger like
> a paper cut.
>
> A beat before
> the blood comes.

Relationships break down in these poems because people fail to connect, to communicate, or to act.

Like the best and most familiar torch songs, many of Jacobs-Beck's poems are infused with a jazz sensibility as evidenced by her use of white space and jagged line breaks. In these spare lyrics white space suggests silence and absence, trademark themes in the torch genre. One may hear the trademark sound, the mesmerizing cry of the saxophone, in the flow of water, in the abundance of water images in this collection, as if the heart could be buoyed in places where "water breaks" and "creeks [roar]" and "rain blows." But renewal is not the symbol here, as human triumph for Jacobs-Beck is hard won.

For all its pitfalls, love is a gamble this poet will take. In "First," the speaker is slow-dancing with her lover, drunk on wine and the pleasures of touching. Looking back she asks, "How could we see where we/ were going to light?" They keep moving, as we all must. We're in it for the duration, body and soul.

Nancy Botkin

## Upper Midwest Love Poem

Summer selfie in
        the South Dakota grass
cumulus and sun shadows
below the blue blue blue
This is now.

        Back then,
I would have walked to Iowa
on callused feet if I
were prairie wild

But no. Wrote out my love
daily, sublimated
        schoolgirl lust,
Find, then lose you, every night.

Now. Beyond the gate,
        golden foxtail and garlic chives

## Back Home

I can feel the lake before I see it
Smell ripples in the wavelight
Hear kelp, feel brown lapping
at the edge, wash sand
leave footprints

Throw paper to the wind
Caution pushed under
the shining surface

Fly from the edge to the center
French saint to French strait
Both shores from the sky
scrapers like Lego towers

Fish among freighters
lake water presses break walls
pounds against borders

*First*

Slightly drunk slow dance,
rhythmic rocking, just breath
on my neck, just hold tight
it must be wine that
makes it right, makes it
tight and sweet.

How could we see where we
          were going to light?

How could we—
How could—
Fall into slushy melt.

## Rumpelstiltskin

Men keep their names
Bad daddies trade

daughters for favor.
Say Rumpelstiltskin. Say it.

My uncles laugh when I refuse.
They think I can't say it

But I can. I know
the tale—the daughter

trapped, imposter under
her father's lie, unable

to spin. I plan my escape
from laughing uncles, teasing

father, a long line of
bullshitters and thieves.

## Skin

We wait in the dark
for answers to form
and float on air.

Skin to skin like magnets.
Bodies tell the truth.

Words are liars—
                    yours are.

My silent anger like
a paper cut.

A beat before
the blood comes.

Precise beaded
line of pain

Skin doesn't lie.
Your body says wait
                    for me.

# Fake Love Spell

## 1. An Old Poem

He swirled tea leaves
in the bottom of his cup,
sipped the quickly
cooling bitterness

"What do you see?" he teased,
pushing the mug
under my face. I looked, then looked
into his eyes, turned to a wasp in amber.

2. A New Poem

I don't even like you—
          you say, sorry you
          feel that way.
          You're crazy, ha.
          Just kidding. Didn't
          mean it.

Squatting incubus
on a sleeping
woman. I can't
writhe free. Days roll
into days, years.

Throw the alarm
clock at me, a
laundry basket
at the child.
Terrify me. I'll clean
up your rage.

Float through it—
peppermint leaves
in a teacup. Mint
breaks spells. Wards
evil. I need
an amulet of
mint to keep you away.

## Damage Sonnet

A note from the teacher started it, some
first grade crime, worse, maybe, than the others.
Now, daily anger turned up an octave,
she packed a small suitcase,
shoved my sister into her little
blue-flowered hooded coat and red boots, made
her sit on the step by the door,
and told her, I'm giving you away.
No.
Please don't.
We will never be the same now.
No.
How can I leave a trail of
pebbles, or breadcrumbs, or bones
so my sister can find her way home?

## Why Are We Here?

Because my ex
my ex, and shackles

Success in a cesspool
Babies are rootballs
Stuck in the swamp
Sink hole
        Suck hole

Dreaming of short grass prairie

## Michigan Women

Tell us how
you really feel

flame     ash

No firewall will save us

Brain tumor grandma
smoking in her hospital bed
what does it matter now

stone     bone

Tongues carved from flint
or petoskey

## Jeremiah Morrow Bridge

The highest in Ohio.
I tighten every time
I drive across,
I feel the poor ghosts
haunting the girders

People say "I can't imagine"
but I can: step off and nothing holds
        acceleration through the green blur
                slam into the muddy Little Miami
                    water breaks
                        and breaks

## One Year

1780s bank house above
a creek. It seems
An Adventure
to live at the end
of a road.

Steep wooden stairs, two flights
and a toddler.

We can't afford oil
to heat three
stories of stone walls.

The furnace shuts off
some nights, pilot light out.
To start it, I go
outside, into frigid moonlight,
city girl afraid among
owls and snakes.

But come on, he said
it will be fun
an adventure

All I hear is the creek roaring
after rain
rising

## Early

On your last night we share
a bed, but don't sleep,
don't make love—we've tried
and failed at both. We are
disappointed in ourselves,
in each other. This week,
we thought, a beginning
to love delayed, has declined
into awkward rhythm. We
talk all night, curled together,
worrying—what's next?
It's getting light outside.
The birds are singing. Stupid birds.

## Train to Montreal in 1980

You'd think, my blond blue-eyed
sweet one
that dozing off
on the CN train, heads
inclined together,
you'd think
(the whispers)
that we'd
you think, from all the noise

I protest,
lie to them
                to you
                            to myself
my head on your shoulder
yes it is
yes

# Colorless Morning

(after *Rose Meditative*, Salvador Dali)

Full bloom red rose
Levitating
like the
Buddha

Lotus peace
Red rose passion
Passion lotus
Peace rose

Honors daughter
Rebel wife
Sacrifice mama

Drive the coastal highway
wild roses light the way

*Because you're hurt, you*

slam
the door while rain
blows through the screen.
Stunned
I stand, then slide
the window closed, the wet curtain
sticks to my skin.

I want to follow you.
I want to
dissolve into your
mouth. If I look
into those hazel-strange eyes,
I will confess: I
dream about your tongue
your forearms and artist fingers.

Instead
I stand still, while thunder
breaks the August sweat,
spell broken and
you're gone.

## *Torch*

Sing "Sunday Kind of Love"
and "Guilty"
      on blast
It's a dry heat
passionate celibacy
smoke, maybe fire

Fall in love on the phone
confess our sins and love of
Etta    Patsy
Billie    Bonnie
requited-but-impossible
      500 miles and
            a marriage

Many nights, long distance
your voice slides into me
touches me the way
your tongue will

so so guilty

## List from 610 Third St.

Remember to buy groceries.
We need
      —plums
      —brie
Oh, and
      —milk.

Remember to pay:
      —electric bill
      —water bill
or we will
      —live like pioneers,
      carrying pails and
      sleeping at sunset.

Remember that you
      —pinned me to the counter
      when we argued,

      —saw a soft spot, a bruise,
      —poked a hole through
      with your thumb.

## Sunday

Most years, too cold for
our candy-colored Easter dresses
        bare legs
                spring coats
we wear them anyway.
The net slip under the skirt
        itches my legs
                red, rough red

All the cousins gather
violets from the grass
in Grandma's backyard,
        fingers cold,
we were called by
pale sunshine,
then called for lunch:
fancy glass plates,
beautiful food that
deceives:
relish tray of pickles and olives
        pimientos
        radish and butter
sandwiches on firm white bread,
creamy and bitter,
        the radishes so rosy
        and crisp white—how
can they taste like pepper and dirt?

## Berry Patch

never did produce
any fruit, just ten feet of thorns and
rich green leaves, so
at your request
I dug it up, all of it
       risked thorns and blisters
because you asked me to
because maybe you
       will notice
berry bushes abortive in
the backyard

## *Maybe*

Goodbye in the garage,
you say, I don't know if this will work,
but keep kissing,
lingering, saying
Gotta go, but
your feet stay still.
Over your shoulder
daffodils glow in the gloom,
on a gray Saturday,
a talisman that tells me
you'll be back, no matter what you say.
You roll down the driveway,
wave with love in your eyes.
The road is long, and I will suffer first.
You'll be back when
my star that guards the gate

Burns right above me.

## Observatory, 09/10/16

I broke Dan's heart
      in the event tent
      under the pin oaks.
A lecture on the lawn
A lightning storm.

Anger covers fear:
      don't astronomers
      understand
      electricity and metal
      poles?

Let's go home. Now. Please.

My sweet introvert
      fills in the small
      talk gap
Struggling with his tongue

Lightning lessens
      before we leave
      our shoes sink into
      the muddy lawn
      as we walk to the car
      seething.

## Monday

Hold on in my red
blouse black
pant suit
like Hillary
campaigning
stump speeching

Silly ceremony—we stand on
sore feet, sensible
heels a disapointment
my mascara smudges
and now what

Can't fail
so much riding
so much
Do. Not. Fuck. It. Up.
so much riding

## Retired Queen

I am past all that now.
I will walk in black woods
trees speak to me,
envy me my range

Time to fade from
spotlight blue to
            candle flicker.
Burning out is
a young man's game

Rust away
from the glaze and glare.
Turn to leaf litter,
            feed the forest
under the rumor of leaves

## For the Bad Sister on Her Birthday

I don't remember any more
than you do. I had a baby
head start on you, fifteen months
of firstborn.

But I know the story:
premature blood
emergency C

That bloody Friday
Dad chose to save Mom

They saved you both
but Mom never forgave you
and you never forgave me
for being first, most beloved

People say it must
be wonderful to have a sister
to grow up with

I don't answer, soap in my mouth
for your lies

## Aunt Sande

My idol with the cool chick apartment
and gold VW Bug.
He took her flame out. Stole my playful aunt.
Eight years old, and I could feel
the cold in him,
the criminal.

Their wedding, a loss.
I rubbed jasmine petals fallen
from her bouquet on my face,
a way to say goodbye.

## Modern Goddess

Hike the concrete path
in search of my bones
buried under weight
too old to be blamed
on pregnancy.

After dinner, the humid
river valley effaces.
March up and down hills
to burn these thighs.

Find flower buds
strewn in my path: Aphrodite
or an ancient bride.
Carry a blossom on my palm
on the dark walk home.

## Detroit Home Movies

Everyone has a
cousin sister aunt Kathy
middle name Marie

hair in curlers and a
crooked-toothed smile she
covers with her hand

hides her face against the fence post
above the coral roses

tugging her prom dress
giggling with the boy
she'll marry

Tigers game blares
from the new tv
a life of diapers
and Stroh's beer cans,
lion scepter crown

## Easter Egg

A hardboiled egg, eaten on Easter
I'm standing at the sink with salt and pepper,
carefully removing the shell, sharp
edges yield to reveal the smooth
white, layer over layer, yolk,
yellow and gray, the core.
This is my Easter ritual,
left over from blessed baskets
filled with food, lining church aisles.
Polish grandmothers fussing
with basket linens, careful to expose each item,
required by tradition—
bread, kielbasa, colored eggs,
salt and pepper, sweets, a butter lamb.
Easter communion. Not the body and blood, transmuted;
real food, to be eaten first thing Easter Sunday.
A meal to break the fast, to break
the day. Break the egg, break with the past,
break the winter dark.

## Scrubbed

Beauty is truth
so tell the truth
creates beauty.

Sometimes beauty flares and crackles
in a moment of confession
sometimes truth comes
in the steam heat
scrubbing so hard
skin turns red, stings
and turns to naked beauty.

Horror brings truth
devastation beauty
all you need to know

# Elegy, for Belva

Every six months, more frail, until
                         a cold January day.
For years, a widow—at last, she was
glad to pass, to be with him again.

Snow in Cedar Rapids.
Buried her under a tree
                         planted 20 years ago
for him, in the yard
of a tiny, musty church.

After, we stand quietly among the cars, outside
                         the churchyard fence,
watch snow blow across fallow
fields under a dry blue sky,

Midwest winter day so sunny
                         the cold's a paradox,
lungs ache with each breath, eyelashes freeze.
A January Iowa goodbye.

Made in the USA
Las Vegas, NV
05 November 2021

33767119R00028